9.75

Let's visit a
CEREAL FARM

Sarah Doughty
and
Diana Bentley
Reading Consultant
University of Reading

Photographs by
Chris Fairclough

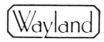

Let's Visit a Farm

Beef Farm
Cereal Farm
Dairy Farm
Fish Farm
Fruit Farm
Market Garden
Pig Farm
Poultry Farm
Sheep Farm

First published in 1990 by
Wayland (Publishers) Ltd
61 Western Road, Hove
East Sussex BN3 1JD, England

© Copyright 1990 Wayland (Publishers) Ltd

British Library Cataloguing in Publication Data
Doughty, Sarah
    Let's visit a cereal farm.
    1. English language – Readers
    I. Title   II. Bentley, Diana
    III. Doughty, Sarah
    Let's visit a farm
    428.6

ISBN 1 85210 747 2

Phototypeset by
Kalligraphics Ltd
Horley, Surrey
Printed and bound by
Casterman S.A., Belgium

Contents

All the words that appear in
bold are explained in the
glossary on page 28.

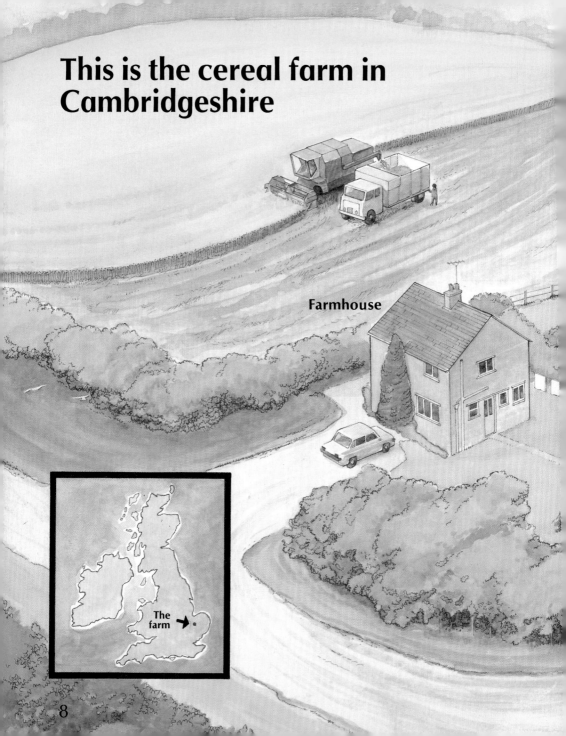

This is the cereal farm in Cambridgeshire

Farmhouse

The farm

8

Storage shed

Barn

9

Here are the cereal farmer and his family

Here are Mr and Mrs Bramley and their children. Mr Bramley is a **cereal** farmer. In many of his fields he grows wheat. Wheat plants produce **grains** which are used to make flour. This can be made into bread, biscuits and breakfast foods.

The farmer ploughs the field and breaks up the soil

Before planting wheat, Mr Bramley ploughs his land. He drives a tractor which pulls the plough across the field. The plough has sharp blades which cut the earth into big pieces and turn it over.

The ground is not yet ready for planting. Seeds need fine soil, so the farmer uses a **harrow** to break up any lumps of earth.

The wheat seeds are planted in the ground

Mr Bramley plants wheat seeds using a seed-drill.
First he puts the seeds in the part of the drill called
the **hopper**. The hopper carries the seeds while they
are being planted.

    The tractor pulls the seed-drill across the field. The
drill plants the seeds in the ground in tidy rows. Each
seed is planted with a little **fertilizer.**

In spring the farmer sprays the wheat crop

By the spring, the green shoots of wheat show above the ground. The farmer wants to protect his **crop** from **pests** and diseases. To do this he sprays the crop with **chemicals**.

The tractor pulls the chemical sprayer across the field. Its long arms unfold and cover the wheat crop. Spraying does not harm the growing wheat plants.

The farmer shows the crop to the children

In the summer, Mr Bramley looks at his crop to check it is healthy and growing well. He shows the plants to the children. Mr Bramley is pleased with the wheat's growth.

The farmer does not want his plants to grow too tall, so he will add a growth **regulator** to his crop.

19

In summer the farmer harvests the wheat

In the summer wheat grains grow at the tips of the long, brown stalks. The grains are protected by a strong **husk**. Mr Bramley looks at the grains to see if they are ripe.

When the wheat is ready to **harvest**, Mr Bramley cuts the crop using a combine harvester. The large wheel at the front of the machine lifts the wheat so the stalks are easy to cut.

The harvester sorts the grain from the stalks

When the wheat is harvested, the grain is separated from the stalks. The combine harvester cuts off the stalks and they fall to the ground. The grain is stored in a tank inside the combine harvester. When this tank is full, the grain is emptied into a trailer.

The stalks of wheat left in the field are called straw. Some farmers tie them into bales. Mr Bramley ploughs his straw back into the field.

The grain is dried in a storage barn

The wheat grains are taken to a storage barn. The grains are tipped out of the trailer and stored on the barn floor. They are dried by fans which blow hot air into the barn.

Mr Bramley sells the dried grains to a **miller**. The miller crushes the grains and makes them into flour.

A farmer has plenty of work to do

A farmer is always busy. All year there are jobs to do around the farm. Sometimes Mr Bramley looks at the ditches which run next to his fields. He makes sure that the water can easily drain away from the land.

Mr Bramley takes good care of his tractor. He checks the machinery and mends any broken parts. Then he can be sure that the tractor will work when it is time to plant and grow next year's crop.

Glossary

Cereal A plant that has small, hard seeds or grains that are used as food.

Chemicals Substances used on plants to improve the crop.

Crop Food plants that are grown in fields.

Fertilizer A substance added to soil to make it richer.

Grains The small, hard seeds of cereal plants.

Harrow A machine that breaks up the earth and levels the ground.

Harvest To pick or gather a crop.

Hopper Part of a seed-drill that carries seeds.

Husk The dry, outside covering of grain.

Miller A person who grinds grain into flour at the mill.

Pests Animals or insects that are harmful to crops.

Regulator A chemical that controls crop growth.

Acknowledgement

The publishers would like to thank the farmer and his family for their help and co-operation in the making of this book.

Books to read

Food and Drink by A. Mountfield (Macmillan, 1988)
Tractors on the Farm by P. Heeks and R. Whitlock
    (Wayland, 1984)
Wheat on the Farm by P. Heeks and R. Whitlock
    (Wayland, 1984)

Places to visit

Notes for parents and teachers

To find out more about visiting a cereal farm, or any other type of farm in your area, you might like to get in touch with the following organizations:

The Association of Agriculture (Farm Visits Service), Victoria Chambers, 16–20 Strutton Ground, London SW1P 2HP.
They have produced a useful booklet called *Farms to Visit in Britain* which gives details of farms that are open to the public, many with special facilities for schools.

The National Union of Farmers, Agriculture House, 25–31 Knightsbridge, London SW1X 7NJ.
Local branches organize visits to farms. Their addresses can be obtained from your library.

County Colleges of Agriculture
These exist in most counties. Many have an established Schools Liaison or Environmental Studies Unit. Contact the Association of Agriculture if you have difficulty in locating your local College of Agriculture.

Index